Narco
Awake O Sleeper

Edie Bayer

ISBN-13: 978-0692330005
ISBN-10: 0692330003

DEDICATED

TO ALL THE CHRISTIANS WHO KNOW IT'S TIME
TO WAKE UP. THEY FEEL IT IN THEIR SPIRIT.
BUT JUST DON'T KNOW HOW.

THIS BOOK IS FOR YOU.

CONTENTS

Acknowledgments   i

Foreword by Darren Canning   iii

Preface   7

1   Awaken Your Gifts   11

2   Awaken to Politics   19

3   Awaken to Relationship   29

4   Awaken to Submission   39

5   Awaken to Love   47

ACKNOWLEDGMENTS

I want to thank my husband, Darryl, for his patience, endurance, love and support. You have an amazing crown awaiting you! You have been my cheerleader and strong tower in the earth realm. Thank you, honey.

I would like to thank Joan Hunter for giving me such an amazing example to follow as an apostle, a prophet and a preacher, besides being just an incredible person. You showed me that it was possible to really stand up and shine as an author and a minister to change lives. Thank you.

I want to thank Pastor Frankie Mazzapica for the many stories that he told while I sat under his teaching. So many of them have stuck with me over these last years, I still refer to them as I minister! Thank you.

I would love to thank Pastor Shawn O'Hearn and Dr. Terry Thompson for the roles they played in shaping me as a Christian. None of us knew then how important those messages were that became so deeply ingrained in me.

THANK YOU.

Edie Bayer

FOREWORD
BY
DARREN CANNING
AUTHOR, MENTOR, PROPHETIC REVIVALIST
WWW.DARRENCANNING.ORG

As I read Edie's words in this book I was struck by the vividness, honesty and fearlessness of her words. She is a veritable John the Baptist preparing the way of the Lord. She is demanding purity to rise in the Land and specifically in the lives of those in the church.

We must always remind ourselves that the world that we see before us is a battlefield. People are fighting on one side or the other. Our greatest weapon in this battle is our ability to love one another. As Christians we must love one another, but we must also love those who are not lovely.

It is easy to love the greatest saint - the ones that look

pure in heart. The Billy Grahams, the Francis of Assisi's, and Teresa of Avila's, but what about the brother and sister who are wrestling with sin or who do not share our individual creeds or brand of Christian identity. It can be harder to love them especially if they are continuously confronting us, but love them we must.

The Father sent us into the world to love one another. I believe Edie is calling the church to love. I believe she is calling you to a higher standard. She is calling you to truth and to Christian purity.

I have spent many hours with Edie and her husband Darryl. They exhibit a true childlike imagination for the things of God and especially for the miracles, signs and wonders that take place in the Kingdom. They have encouraged me greatly and have challenged me to also believe for the greater things.

It is an honour for me to write the foreword to this book. Read it with an open heart and be prepared to be challenged from complacency.

God bless you all,

Darren Canning
Canada. 2014

Darren Canning Ministries
www.darrencanning.org

Narco – Awake O Sleeper

Narco – Awake, O Sleeper

Preface

Everywhere we look we see signs of the times. The Lord has His hand on us, yet somehow we feel uneasy and distant, not at ease and comforted any longer.

That is how you know you are awakening.

Once upon a time, in a land far, far away, we were able to rest easy. That is simply not the case any longer. September 11. Another earthquake, another bomb threat, another hijacking, another terrorist attack somewhere. Hamas. Isis. I hear everywhere another prophetic voice has an AWAKEN message, or songs by worship leaders beckoning us to arise and shine, for our light has come.

Jesus said to work while it is still daylight because the night is coming and no one will be able to work.

That is why the Lord has prompted me to write this book about waking up. He specifically told me to write a book and call it "Narco". Honestly, I thought He wanted me to write about pharmaceutical drugs. I responded by telling the Lord I can't write a book about drugs! I don't know enough about them!

After a while I knew that He didn't want me to write about drugs. That is when I began to research the word itself, "NARCO". Since God hides many meanings in the names of things I looked up the etymology of the word. "NARCO" is the root of *Narcotics* which is why I thought the Lord wanted me to write a book about pharmaceutical drugs. However, in my research, I discovered it is the root of not only *Narcotics*, but of *Narcolepsy, Narcosis* and many other sleep-related words.

The root word "NARCO" means to lull to sleep. It's origins are from the Greek word *narke*, meaning numbness; *narkoo*, meaning "I put to sleep". It also means "stupor", "narcosis", and finally, "sleep".

I soon realized that God wanted me to write a book to His children about *WAKING UP OUT OF OUR STUPOR!*

The children of God must wake up and unite. That is the only way we will be able to win the war on our souls … and that of our children.

That is the reason for this book. To learn HOW to wake up, TO WHAT, and WHAT TO DO once you are awake.

The Bride of Christ is awakening from her slumber – and she is You.

1 Corinthians 15:51-53 (NKJV) [51] *Behold, I tell you a mystery: We shall not all sleep, but we shall all be changed—* [52] *in a moment, in the twinkling of an eye, at the last trumpet. For the trumpet will sound, and the dead will be raised incorruptible, and we shall be changed.*

Edie Bayer

Chapter 1

Awaken Your Gifts

What is a gift? Is it a package with some wrapping paper and a bow?

Yes. But this kind is special. It's from your Daddy.

There will come a time in your walk with God that you will realize that He has given gifts. Either you will recognize them in someone else, or they will be recognized in you.

Personally, I realized that I had a "prophetic anointing" when it was told to me by a former Pastor. I was in a meeting with some of the other leadership of the church and talked about a vision I had. I will never forget how she stared at me, as if she was using X-Ray vision to see into my soul! She told me that she thought I had a prophetic anointing, and in a later conversation she said that what we DO as prophets is sometimes just *"throw it against the wall and see if it sticks"*!

I had absolutely no idea what she meant THEN. I sure do now.

I remember some of those early first prophetic words as I unwrapped my gift from Daddy over the next few years -- the gift of prophecy. Literally, just like a child learning to speak, some "goo-goos" and "ga-gas" came out of my mouth. But soon, these early prophetic words started to formulate and make sense. Just as a baby becomes a toddler and begins to gain control of his mouth and tongue, those unintelligible sounds start to string together. At first there is just gibberish, then actual sounds, then words, and finally whole sentences.

In the beginning, I remember talking to a friend of mine about this process. I said that God literally only gave me A WORD -- just ONE WORD.

She told me, "Don't worry, He'll give you more. That's a good start!"

She was right! Now He gives me whole sermons, messages, blog-posts and books. And He will do it for you, too.

So, that is where we start. First you have to WANT the gifts that God gives, then believe He will give them to you. Actually first you have to KNOW that God gives gifts. Then you have to WANT them, then Believe that your Daddy God will give them to you.

Paul talks about prophecy as a gift in **1 Corinthians 14, vs. 1-5** and that we should covet it, or desire it. His reasoning? Because Prophecy EDIFIES, or builds up the church.

I have noticed that when I am prophesying over someone that God will not let me speak negatively *TO* them or *ABOUT* them. It's amazing! I may know something negative is going on in their life, maybe not specifics, but SOMETHING. God will turn the thought process around, the entire sentence structure, to say something positive and uplifting.

As an example, let's say in the course of prophesying to an individual that I realize this person has a challenge s/he is overcoming, either spiritually, relationally or physically. In this example, I may think, "You are having family problems right now."

BUT GOD...the way He will cause it to come out of my mouth will be uplifting and encouraging, such as, "God is helping you to overcome some obstacles to win the victory in your family!" or, "God is working behind the scenes to eliminate the obstacles that the enemy has placed before you. Hang in there! It won't be long!"

See? His goal is to help his children WALK OUT of that situation, and into the thing that He has for them. God will not beat anybody down with a prophetic word.

The most negative Word I have ever received was directly to ME! It's true. You can read about it in my blog, "*God's Notes*" (**http://ediebear1.wordpress.com**) . In it I actually heard God SIGH. He was giving me instructions --- I just wasn't obeying. He was not speaking rapidly ---I just wasn't listening.

At that moment I didn't realize how important what He was saying was. Since that time I have learned that the nuances of His whispered voice mean EVERYTHING.

Generally speaking, and I am talking about prophetic words, if it is negative it isn't from God. That is not *always* true -- there are truly words of correction -- but those are for the body to TURN AROUND. If someone walks up to you with a word and starts to degrade you or abrade you, it's not God. Now, that's not to say that you will never hear anything you don't WANT to hear….but God will never hurt you with a prophetic word. He will try to steer you away from something, and He will always show you the bright side.

Now, let's talk about some of God's other GIFTS.

The gifts that God gives to us are listed in **1 Corinthians 12:4-11**: *4 Now there are distinctive varieties and distributions of endowments (gifts, [a]extraordinary powers distinguishing certain Christians, due to the power of divine grace operating in their souls by the Holy Spirit) and they vary, but the [Holy] Spirit remains the same.*

5 And there are distinctive varieties of service and ministration, but it is the same Lord [Who is served].

6 And there are distinctive varieties of operation [of working to accomplish things], but it is the same God Who inspires and energizes them all in all.

7 But to each one is given the manifestation of the [Holy] Spirit [the evidence, the spiritual illumination of the Spirit] for good and profit.

8 To one is given in and through the [Holy] Spirit [the power to speak] a message of wisdom, and to another [the power to express] a word of knowledge and understanding according to the same [Holy] Spirit;

9 To another [[b]wonder-working] faith by the same [Holy] Spirit, to another the extraordinary powers of healing by the one Spirit;

10 To another the working of miracles, to another prophetic insight ([c]the gift of interpreting the divine will and purpose); to another the ability to discern and distinguish between [the utterances of true] spirits [and false ones], to another various kinds of [unknown] tongues, to another the ability to interpret [such] tongues.

11 All these [gifts, achievements, abilities] are inspired and brought to pass by one and the same [Holy] Spirit, Who apportions to each person individually [exactly] as He chooses.

Now, the reason I brought this up is because YOU have gifts too. We all do! God isn't going to give **me** gifts without giving **you** gifts! God loves both of us equally, because we are both His favorites! So, you have gifts just like I have gifts, just like Timothy had gifts.

You simply need to AWAKEN them.

How do you do this? By stirring up the gift that is within you!

And how do you stir up the gifts? The Bible says in **1 Timothy 1: 6-7**: " *6 Therefore I remind you to stir up the gift of God which is in you through the laying on of my hands. 7 For God has not given us a spirit of fear, but of power and of love and of a sound mind.*"

So, Paul is telling Timothy how to stir up HIS OWN gift. Paul is speaking to Timothy, his son in the faith. He is telling Timothy that Timothy has a gift within himself, and that gift that is now inside Timothy was imparted into him when Paul put his hands on him.

By gosh, if Paul can do it, we can do it, too!!

You will stir yours up in the same way! It's easy! Just put your hands on your belly, and DECLARE that you are stirring up the gifts within you! Repeat after me:

"I shall prophesy! I shall speak in other tongues! I have the Gift of Faith! I have miracle working power! I have Gifts of Healings! I speak words of Wisdom! I speak Words of Knowledge! I discern spirits! I interpret tongues!"

It is really just that simple. Write it down on a sheet of paper, and tape it to the bathroom mirror. Rinse, repeat. Every morning and every evening, and every time you use the rest room throughout the day. Every time you wash your hands. That should be at least 20-30 times a day!

The other way to stir up your gift is to USE IT!

Oh, I know, now I am stretching you! You MUST use a muscle in order for it to become strong...right? You MUST use your gifts for them to become strong.

So, prophesy! Speak in Tongues! Lay hands on the sick! Discern spirits! USE YOUR FAITH!

Can you imagine what you would do if you KNEW that when you laid hands on someone they would recover? Wouldn't you go from hospital to hospital, from the morgue to the streets to the schools?

What if you KNEW something about someone that they desperately WANTED to know – or need to know? About their situation now, or about their future? Everyone wants to know the future!

What if whatever you believe for came true???

These are the gifts that the Father has given to us, His children. Instead of unwrapping a bicycle on Christmas morning, your Father has given you 9-different gifts that that you can open anytime you want! These gifts make you SUPERNATURAL, and they have from the beginning of time.

 Faith that makes your words become reality. Speaking words of life to others that they desperately need to hear. Touching people and they are healed. Miracles that occur everywhere you go. Being able to tell good spirits from bad, and which spirit is what. Understanding and speaking wisdom.   Knowing something about a person that makes them see that it MUST be God, that there is no humanly possible way that you could know that information about them!

All you have to do is believe like a little child. And awaken this child inside of you, awaken your gifts.

Chapter 2

Awaken to Politics

This chapter may seem a little harsh, reprimanding and scolding.

It is.

God scolded ME! I am just His mouthpiece.

Not everyone will read this book, or maybe even this particular chapter. There are plenty more people just like me, writing feverishly to the audience that God has for them. God is using us to get His people to turn away from self-idolatry, back to Him, to become the chosen vessels that HE is using to forward His Kingdom Plan and Purposes.

This chapter will be supernaturally written by God. Why? Because I know nothing about politics! I don't follow politics, as a rule, I never have.

But I realized it is time I woke up to the fact that I have to help run this country, and you do too!

I do know that as Christians, we need to WAKE UP and take back what was once ours, that which in our apathy and laziness – or simply in our busy-ness or in our trusting-ness --- we simply let slip away.

We used to OWN this place. It was OURS. I want it back. And I need your help.

And that means that we need to take back the political arena. We need to take back the seats of power, the mountain of Government. We need to wake up to the fact that every demonic power and principality in this realm is working toward our demise. The other team is trying to eliminate us, silence us, put us in handcuffs and if that doesn't work, BEHEAD US.

We have allowed all of this to happen. The people of God have allowed our own freedoms to slip away, out of our grasps. We allowed the gays to have the right to marry, by not putting down the gay revolution of the 1960's and 1970's. As Christians, we were too NICE, and we didn't want to hurt anybody in the name of Love.

About the same as kissing a snake, we figured it wouldn't hurt us, didn't impact us, as long as it didn't bite. We didn't realize that we empowered it by not fighting it. Like a giant pimple that needed to be popped, but we didn't and now it is huge, scabbed over, a giant pustule, red and angry and infected – now it will take a whole lot more work to get it healthy again…and there will ALWAYS be a scar.

Those days of doing nothing are behind us. We need to wake up, shake off the apathy and/or sheer busy-ness of our lives and get out there and VOTE. We need to become familiar with the issues, as many as we can possibly get a hold of with our own two hands – the same two hands we use to vote! We need to have Christian politicians in office. We need to get Christians involved in politics from the inside out. We need to become part of the Tea Party.

We need to stand up for the Bible, for God and for Family. NO MATTER WHAT HAPPENS TO US. We need to be ready to be persecuted, because of our lack of doing anything at all in the past.

I am as guilty as anyone else. I didn't even vote, except for Ross Perot, until after 9/11. I didn't even vote for the first time until I was in my 40's! Since that fateful day, when all that we knew as a country in a bubble was ripped out of our clutches, I have voted in every election that I can. I may not know all the agendas of all the players … as just one person, who can keep up with all that shifting sand? However, I DO trust certain groups that know all the agendas of all the players, and I rely on them to do my homework for me.   It's the very best I can do, at least for now. I praise God that these groups even formed to help us!

I love the bumper stickers that say, "I'm Catholic, and I VOTE!" Take that, liberals! I may not be a fan of Catholicism, but I can count on the Catholics to vote Pro-Life! And generally speaking, most pro-life candidates have Christian values. So at least we vote the same, even if we don't believe the same.

This whole thing with insurance and Hobby Lobby and the Catholic Church and the fight over birth control and abortion pills….who would have EVER thought that America, the land of the free, would sink to this level? Talk about lowering yourself to the level of your enemy! We have sunk into the muck and mire of the vomit of dogs.

How on earth did the liberals get control of this country?

Butterfly!

That's right, Butterfly. That's how. We were distracted. By something. That is how the enemy gets us, with distraction. That is how we get suckered into arguments, into sin, and that is how we have lost control of the rule and the reign of this country and indeed the planet.

Distracted. In fact, that is how we have lost control of our morals in this country, by being distracted. While we were distracted with (whatever) the enemy moved in. Not all at once, but little by little, he snuck in.

While we weren't looking (butterfly) he enacted a law. While we weren't looking (butterfly), gays were allowed to adopt children. While we weren't looking (butterfly) filth and debasement became the norm in music and while we weren't looking (butterfly), Christianity became a bad word and a byword, something to be despised and looked down upon, frowned at and not allowed any more.

(Butterfly) We cannot speak of God in our public schools. (Butterfly) We cannot talk about God in the workplace. (Butterfly) No more Merry Christmas!

Meanwhile, the city of Houston has a special interest group Mayor who has enacted legislature that says it's ok for men to use women's bathrooms, and women to use men's bathrooms in the city of Houston.

What kind of insanity is this?

It's the kind that the enemy wanted, the kind that we weren't looking out for, the kind the Bible warns us about, the Sodom and Gomorrah of the 21st century.

God Help Us Help Ourselves!

Lord, wake us up! Shake us up! Lord, we know Your plans and purposes are to bless us and not to harm us. We know You have plans, which if we worked WITH you and didn't interfere would work for us, and not against us … unlike the plans of the enemy.

Oh, you didn't know the enemy has plans too?

Everything he does is a mimicry of what God does. God has plans and purposes and tells us so in Jeremiah 29:11. Guess what? So does the enemy. He has plans and purposes to harm us, and NOT to bless us, to take away our hope and our future.

But we can't blame it all on the enemy! We do make choices.

Look at Deuteronomy 28. There are 2-pages of blessings, absolutely everything you would ever need in life contained in verses 1-14 when you obey the voice of the Lord, walk in His ways and heed His voice. Then, in verses 15 onward Deuteronomy tells us this is what happens when we DON'T obey the voice of the Lord our God.

Catch this! The Lord tells us if we CHOOSE not to listen and obey what will happen. 5-pages of curses follow after that.

He told us to choose, and choose life. But what did we do? We chose...

Butterfly!

Looks a lot like the United States of America is starting to form around the infection doesn't it? A pus pocket, covered in a scab...and we get to live in it.

Or do we?

We CAN change it. All we have to do is backtrack through time, take back the rights that we have given away, and take back all the territory the enemy has stolen. It's simple. Start over again.

Well, ok. It's SIMPLE. I didn't say it would be easy! We cannot do anything without God. And without unity. That is why we are to love one another as Christians.

It's about unity. Because one can put a thousand to flight, and two can put ten-thousand to flight. That is why the devil is working his absolute hardest to keep us from getting together with one common cause. Because there is not only safety in numbers, there is STRENGTH.

We have to come to grips with the fact that the enemy

has effectively fractured us, with over 30,000 denominations, much like God split us all apart with the tower of Babel. In **Genesis 11:6**, *"And the Lord said, Behold, they are one people and they have* [a]*all one language; and this is only the beginning of what they will do, and now nothing they have imagined they can do will be impossible for them."*

In unity, we have untold, unimaginable strength. But we need to use that strength for good, and not for evil.

I keep using homosexuals as my example, because the enemy is using them right now in his battle-plan. They are an excellent example. Simply because they are HOMOSEXUAL they band together effectively. They don't nitpick and fight over whether they are male or female or black or Asian, or if they make money or don't or if they are lesbian or bi-sexual or transsexual or whatever other perversion they prefer. Their god is their FLESH - themselves and sexuality, and they join together – effectively – to further that cause.

And they have been extremely successful.

If only we could overlook all the little tiny flaws in our doctrine and personalities and band together and use our Godly strength in unity to enact good!

You see, we CAN. We just don't. Why?

My guess is PRIDE. Just plain old stinky pride, the "somebody's got to be right, and it's me" kind of pride. The kind of pride that God detests. Yes. That is why we cannot successfully band together.

Or at least we haven't so far.

BUT GOD. He is working to change all that. That is why He has made our common cry "UNITY" for the last few years, because that is His heart's cry. That is why our cry is now "AWAKEN!" --- for the same reason.

Hearken to the heart's cry of the Lord.

Wake up, get out there and VOTE! I have.

Edie Bayer

Chapter 3

Awaken to Relationship

Notice I didn't say "Relationships". I am not talking about personal relationships, although it includes that. I am speaking of RELATIONSHIP with the Father, with the Son and with the Holy Spirit of God.

In relationship, we say "Abba", our Father. We call Jesus our brother as well as our Lord and Savior. Then there is Holy Spirit. He is not THE Holy Spirit, as if He is a THING! It's not possible to have a relationship with a THING, is it? It is only possible to have relationship with the person of Holy Spirit.

Holy Spirit is His Name. He is fully one-third of the

Trinity, one-third of the Godhead, and He lives in YOU! You don't want a THING inside of you, right? We don't want to live in a horror movie!

The truth is He is an amazing part of your walk with Lord Jesus. He is your witness, your guide, your friend. He is your comforter and he is your paraclete – "the one who comes alongside".

I heard an illustration of this once. As the story was told, a soldier was walking along with a very heavy backpack. It was so very heavy, and he was so tired that he was having trouble carrying it. Another soldier came up and took the backpack off his comrade's shoulders, carrying it for the first soldier. He didn't just help him with it, he took the burden on himself. This is a picture of our beloved "paraclete", the HELPER, the one who comes alongside -- to help bear your burdens.

In fact, He carries them for you!

How close can you get in a relationship? Closer than INSIDE of you? A Mother knows that level of closeness, the kind of closeness developed during pregnancy. The intimacy of the embryo growing inside her belly, a fetus that as it grows becomes part of her body, part of her heart, part of her life, part of her being—part of her identity. When something happens to her child, a Mother KNOWS.

My mother thinks about me and I call her. I text my son and he shows up with a surprise visit from out of town! Something goes on in my daughter's life, and without benefit of a text, an email or a phone call I awaken in the middle of the night to pray and intercede for her.

There is a connection between a mother and a child, more than a physical connection, one that supercedes this natural realm.

That is a picture of our relationship with our Father, our heavenly Father, Abba, Daddy God. He lives inside of us. He put His divine sperm, Holy Spirit, inside of us, to grow us into the likeness of Jesus Christ.

1 Peter 1:23 *You have been regenerated (born again), not from a mortal origin (seed, **sperm**), but from one that is immortal by the ever living and lasting Word of God.*

1 John 3:9 *No one born (begotten) of God [deliberately, knowingly, and habitually] practices sin, for God's nature abides in him [His principle of life, the divine **sperm**, remains permanently within him]; and he cannot practice sinning because he is born (begotten) of God.*

Through Holy Spirit, just like with my Mother, when God thinks of us, we call Him – we PRAY! There is a divine, supernatural connection between Abba Father and His children. We know His thoughts. We have his mind.

1 Cor 2:16 *But **we have the mind of Christ** (**the** Messiah) and do hold **the** thoughts (feelings and purposes) **of** His heart.*

*This is **RELATIONSHIP**.* It is far more than mouthing some words from a piece of paper at Christmas out of tradition, or sitting on a bench on a Sunday morning and wishing you were at the golf course.

Relationship with God is what He desires, and what we crave. He created Adam to walk with Him in the cool of the day. We were made for fellowship with the Most High God.   We long for the closeness of a relationship with God, for Him to fill the void that only He can – because he created it.

We call that a "Jesus-shaped hole." It is a hole that only Jesus can fill.

Sadly, until we meet God face to face, we try to fill that hole with so many other things … sometimes alcohol, sometimes drugs, sometimes sex, sometimes darker things. But, when we finally hear the Voice of the One Who can fill that void with what it was intended to contain, we realize that we have mistakenly been chasing shadows.

He wants that contact, that relationship, the intimacy of

a relationship with you. A REAL relationship, one where you know Him for Who He truly is, and not who religion says He is.

He already knows YOU. He has since before you were born! In **Jer. 1:5** God says *"Before I formed you in the womb I knew you,…"* **Psalm 139:13** says, *"For You did form my inward parts; You did knit me together in my mother's womb."*

The Lord has known you since before the beginning of time.

I know that's really hard for us to wrap our brain around, but the key here is AROUND. We think of time as an extremely long line, with a beginning and an end. Time is actually CIRCULAR (or round), eternal, a circle with no beginning and no end.   And God actually lives outside of this circle! He exists outside of time, at least outside of time as we know it.

However, this is not a lesson in Kronos and Kairos. The point is that God DESIGNED YOU to be in relationship with Him, and Him only. He designed you to be His bride, and He wants you. He wants to be intimate with you, in the same way as a husband is intimate in the knowledge of his wife. Not in the sexual sense, but at the level of intimacy ONLY a married couple can know one another.

My friend Darren Canning, in speaking of his relationship with his wife Lydia, says that they can have an entire conversation across the room without saying a word, just by nods, eye movements and facial expressions. Most married couples can relate.

This is where God wants to be with you, in such a close relationship that all He has to do is nod, and you will know what He is saying; He will guide you with His eye. **Psalm 32:8** KJV says, "*I will instruct thee and teach thee in the way which thou shalt go: I will guide thee with mine eye.*" He doesn't want us begging Him for instruction, crying, and screaming because we don't know what he wants. He longs for us to hear His still small voice, to have His mind on every matter.

He WANTS us to be that close to him -- in such a close relationship that we know what He wants us to do. In fact, I just heard somewhere that God wants us to do what we think He would do, not necessarily wait for three confirmations of a request. However, if you are like HIM you will act like Him and make decisions like Him, decisions that are like His.

That only comes by being with Him.

How do you get there? First of all, you have to get married. Not to another human being, but to GOD. In order to be married to Him, you must forsake all others!

That means giving up all the other gods that currently take up your time, attention, affections and resources. This could be just about anything, but primarily whatever you give the BULK of your attention.

If you spend most of your time dreaming of the latest fashions, crawl the mall with every spare moment, and spend every available extra penny on shoes and clothing and seem to never be able to tithe or give offerings – that might just be a god in your life.

If you think about eating all the time, go to church primarily because it means that you can go eat afterward, are hungry constantly, or eat until you are ready to burst so consistently that you are grossly obese, you might just be serving another god -- the god of gluttony.

If you spend most of your hours thinking of fishing, and every weekend on your boat on the river or lake, even though your family is at church...you might just be serving another god.

See, it could be anything, but whatever you cherish or value more than God is a god. That is IDOLATRY.

Anything that you value or cherish more than Him will get in the way of your relationship with Him. Even good things that He gives you, like your children. Your job.

Your spouse. If they come before Him, consistently...
you may be serving another god.

That is the purpose of FASTING, to purposely discipline
your appetites and cravings, to show yourself that you
love, honor and cherish God even more than the food
that your body needs to survive.

Of course, you can fast anything, from Dr. Pepper to TV
to food. I knew a man one time who fasted his lunches
while his young son was in the hospital, much as David
did while his child with Bathsheba lay dying. This man's
child lived.

Treat your relationship with God as the thing of highest
value in your existence. He will become so important to
you that you would rather do anything than to hurt Him.
If you treat your marriage to the Most High as your top
priority, the thing that is Highest importance on your list,
you will be walking in Favor with God in the cool of the
day --- and in the Heat of Battle!

The whole point of awakening to your relationship with
God is to walk closely with the Father. To breathe as He
breathes, to see as He sees, to want what He wants and
to do what He wants done, on earth as it is in heaven.
To WANT to know Him, to WANT to be in love with Him.

I believe that's relationship.

Awaken to your relationship with Him today.

Edie Bayer

Chapter 4

Waking up to Submission

There's that word again! Submission. Brings up images of the ball and chain, doesn't it?

The truth is, submission is the opposite of rebellion, and rebellion is as the sin of witchcraft. Witchcraft is bondage, therefore rebellion is bondage! Submission truly is freedom.

1 Samuel 15:23Amplified Bible (AMP)

23 For rebellion is as the sin of witchcraft, and stubbornness is as idolatry and teraphim (household good luck images).

Here's the Webster's 1828 definition:

"SUBMISSION, n. [L. submissio, from submitto.]

1. The act of submitting; the act of yielding to power or authority; surrender of the person and power to the control or government of another.
2. Acknowledgment of inferiority or dependence; humble or suppliant behavior.
In all submission and humility,
3. Acknowledgment of a fault; confession or error.
4. Obedience; compliance with the commands or laws of a superior.
5. Resignation; a yielding of one's will to the will or appointment of a superior without murmuring."

A. Yield.
B. Acknowledge inferiority or dependence.
C. Obedience.
D. All of the above.

Proverbs 3:5-6 (AMP)

Lean on, trust in, and be confident in the Lord with all your heart and mind and do not rely on your own insight or understanding.

Submitting is not losing. It's winning. It's not a matter

of who is right and who is wrong, like some elementary-school playground argument. It's becoming aware of the fact that you are not know-all, do-all, end-all and that you NEED God to be that in your life.

It is being aware that God IS the Know-All, Do-All, End-All, Alpha, Omega and everything in between. He knows everything and you don't.

God wrote the Book! So let Him be God, because you're not.

You don't even have to be ok with it, just do it!

James 4: 7 (AMP)

> So be subject (submit) to God. Resist the devil [stand firm against him], and he will flee from you.

What if you didn't submit? Even if you resisted the enemy but did not submit he is not required to flee, which he MUST do when you submit to God and to His plans for your life. If you submit to God and resist him, the enemy will have no foot hold, no way to keep you in bondage.

Ephesians 4:26-27 (AMP)

> When angry, do not sin; do not ever let your wrath (your exasperation, your fury or indignation) last

until the sun goes down.

Leave no [such] room or foothold for the devil [give no opportunity to him].

If we are just obedient to the Lord, and do as He asks us to do, we will be in a much better position – that of sons and daughters of the Most High!

Remember, Jesus said in **John 14:20-24** (AMP) :

"20 At that time [when that day comes] you will know [for yourselves] that I am in My Father, and you [are] in Me, and I [am] in you.

21 The person who has My commands and keeps them is the one who [really] loves Me; and whoever [really] loves Me will be loved by My Father, and I [too] will love him and will show (reveal, manifest) Myself to him. [I will let Myself be clearly seen by him and make Myself real to him.]

22 Judas, not Iscariot, asked Him, Lord, how is it that You will reveal Yourself [make Yourself real] to us and not to the world?

23 Jesus answered, If a person [really] loves Me, he will keep My word [obey My teaching]; and My Father will love him, and We will come to him and make Our home (abode, special dwelling place) with him.

24 Anyone who does not [really] love Me does not observe and obey My teaching. And the teaching which you hear and heed is not Mine, but [comes] from the Father Who sent Me.

Listen, the bottom line is we MUST submit to the Lord, to each other, to authority. Frankly, a lot of the problems we have in America today are from not submitting and living Biblically. As a woman, I can specifically state that for the most part women in America are in rebellion. We do not honor and respect our husbands, and a lot of times they cow-tow to us. That is NOT biblical. Good for us, bad for our country. Men are brought up to know to say, "Yes Dear, No Dear" to keep the peace, and it's a JOKE. Biblically, it's just WRONG.

Do I WANT to live like an ancient Hebrew woman, who has to sit outside on the ground while the husband and his friends eat first? NO. But I believe that if women would live more biblically, then men would too. If we just paid attention to the scripture that says,

Ephesians 5:22-31 (AMP)

22 Wives, be subject (be submissive and adapt yourselves) to your own husbands as [a service] to the Lord.

23 For the husband is head of the wife as Christ is the Head of the church, Himself the Savior of [His] body.

²⁴ As the church is subject to Christ, so let wives also be subject in everything to their husbands.

Then the men would also pay attention to this scripture,

²⁵ Husbands, love your wives, as Christ loved the church and gave Himself up for her,

²⁶ So that He might sanctify her, having cleansed her by the washing of water with the Word,

²⁷ That He might present the church to Himself in glorious splendor, without spot or wrinkle or any such things [that she might be holy and faultless].

²⁸ Even so husbands should love their wives as [being in a sense] their own bodies. He who loves his own wife loves himself.

²⁹ For no man ever hated his own flesh, but nourishes and carefully protects and cherishes it, as Christ does the church,

³⁰ Because we are members (parts) of His body.

³¹ For this reason a man shall leave his father and his mother and shall be joined to his wife, and the two shall become one flesh.

Finally, **Ephesians 5:33 (AMP)**

³³ However, let each man of you [without exception] love his wife as [being in a sense] his very own self; and let

the wife see that she respects and reverences her husband [[a]that she notices him, regards him, honors him, prefers him, venerates, and esteems him; and [b]that she defers to him, praises him, and loves and admires him exceedingly].

Jesus loves women. The first Evangelist was a woman! Jesus watched women and told stories about women. He respected women and honored them. God used a woman to bring His Son to earth.

 Jesus loves men, too, sons and daughters of the Most High God. It was His idea that Man and Woman were to be created equal, that we walked TOGETHER, in unison. After all,

Amos 3:3Amplified Bible (AMP)

[3] Do two walk together except they make an appointment and have agreed?

We have an appointment with Destiny, with our Father in Heaven, and with each other.

It is a NOW SEASON to awaken to submission – to submit to authority, submit to one another and submit to God. The time is to Awaken is Now. There won't be another time quite like this one. So Submit.

Edie Bayer

Chapter 5

Awakening to Love

There is an old Henry Fonda and Lucille Ball movie, called "Yours, Mine and Ours" (1968). The premise of the movie is that a man and woman got married that have a LOT of children from previous marriages. Once wed, they have 18 children altogether under one roof and she is ready to give birth to number 19. Toward the end of the movie, the oldest daughter's boyfriend is trying to convince her to have sex with him – it is the 60's, after all, drugs, love, sex and rock and roll.

There is a famous speech at this juncture in the story where Henry Fonda tells her,
> *"If you want to know what love really is, take a look around you. It's giving life that counts. Until you're*

*ready for it, all of the rest is just a big fraud....Life
isn't a "love in", it's the dishes and the orthodontist
and the shoe repairman and ground round instead of
roast beef. And I'll tell you something else: It isn't
going to bed with a man that proves you're in love
with him, it's getting up in the morning and facing
the drab, miserable, wonderful everyday world with
him that counts."*

For the early years of my life this was my definition of
LOVE. It was meeting someone that you want to spend
your life with in this "drab, everyday world" that we live
in. It wasn't a Cinderella existence that I had imagined. I
had watched my mother and father stay married
through thick and thin, the tennis club life, then two jobs
each, poverty, homelessness, surgery, children,
alcoholism and everything else. But they had stayed
married.

So, when I got married to my first husband at 19 ½ and
5-months pregnant this is what I expected. Not happily-
ever-after, but FOREVER, no-matter-what, literally "'til
death do us part", just like the minister said.

But my daughter's father had come from a broken
home, the child of a divorced-and-then-remarried
mother, whose father was promiscuous and had an
adulterous affair with his secretary, who to his credit he
later married. (Interestingly enough, his mother later
married her boss, too!)

My first husband worked diligently to become just like his father, in every way, successful in his field of business, suave, smart and handsome. And when I say in EVERY WAY, I mean it --- Although I didn't realize it.

In fact, a friend of mine had to pull me aside and tell me, at the risk of our friendship, that I didn't see him cheating on me – with an employee! Just like Dad.

He was a restaurant manager, and she was one of the waitresses. Following in his father's footsteps, he later married her! Of course, later he divorced her and married someone else, but I was already many years into my second marriage at that point as well.

So, after all this, mother and dad had a little rougher time, because now they had seen two marriages dissolve – first my sister's, then mine in that order, and each of us had children. This introduced the idea of DIVORCE into the family. When my daughter's father and I separated, I moved back in with mom and dad and began my life over again.

Looking back, I never realized the amount of strain that put on my parents' marriage. I wasn't thinking about them, really. I was thinking about myself, and my young daughter, and my life.

After a little while I was reintroduced to dating, which was totally bizarre, and my parents became "built-in babysitters" (a title my mother later gave it). But having semi-adult children move back into their home with children of their own must have been an incredible amount of stress, tension and hassle for them. Not to mention the responsibility or the cost. But they stuck it out, and my parents are STILL married today! In fact, they just celebrated their 55th year together last September. Double-Grace!

Even with all of that, my idea of love is different now. I have awakened to Love, based on the sacrificial giving of Jesus Christ. He gave His Life for me so that I could have Life.

I have been awakened to love by loving my siblings until it hurts, even when I don't like them. I have three siblings, two brothers and a sister. I love them. I don't always like them. Of course, they don't always like me, either! But I choose to love them, to pray for them, to wish them Happy Birthday and invite them to holiday get-togethers even when I haven't heard from them in months, or in one case, for years. It doesn't matter. We are called to love one another, and I do love them.

I have been awakened to love by humbling myself for the sake of unity, for the sake of family, for the sake of the cross. I have a brother who is holding an offense against me. Unbeknownst to me I said something to his daughter a few years ago that offended him, and so he refuses to speak to me. I have contacted him and apologized, repented and asked him for his forgiveness. However, it is deep-seated and has a strong-hold, so is probably rooted in a lie that he believes that was told to him by the enemy. I recently humbled myself to apologize again and to honor my mother and father by asking him and his family to our Thanksgiving dinner. He said they were going to be out of town, but I suggested that we might be able to get together another time. He hasn't responded yet, but I will continue to humble myself for the sake of unity and family and try to be a repairer of the breach.

I have been awakened to love by honoring my father and my mother, even when they do crazy stuff that makes no sense at all. I still honor them because it's important to them. There are several stories here, but the funniest one is recently they decided to paint the window frames, all the sashes and trim and the front door of their house – PUMPKIN ORANGE. I pulled up in their driveway about a month ago and I think I still have a black-and-blue spot on my chin where my jaw dropped and hit my chest. They have a very cute, redwood-stain sided house that now has bright orange trim. So I walked inside and the first words out of my dad's mouth were, "Did you see our paint job, Missy?" They were so proud! To honor them I just smiled and nodded, agreed with them and told them that I was glad they were happy with it!

I have been awakened to love for the sake of the covenant. I have lived this one out over the last five years, as I have learned what it really means to be in covenant with God and with His people.

It's working and pushing through even when all energy left hours before. Working at the ministry for sometimes over 60 hours a week really tests my love factor! When one is tired, it's so easy to just give up, or to be irritable, or to want to hide in a closet somewhere and just be in the dark and the peace and the quiet, to want to go home and go to bed....this list is endless. However, awakening to love and walking in love means that I work in excellence and keep working in excellence, as if I am working for God Himself, and keep going, no matter what.

Being awakened to love means realizing I CAN'T get into an argument, even when "the old man" resurrects himself and I feel myself "bow-up". Sometimes it would be so easy to open my mouth and just flesh out.

I have a great story about the fruit of the Spirit -- LOVE! My neighbors across the street were partying and drinking with loud music and all that goes with it. I was working late that night on the computer, and as the hour became later and later I realized they were still going. I noticed them at 8:00, then 8:30 then 9:00. About 9:20 I started praying and believing they were going to quit by 10:00 PM, which is the law. 10:00 PM came, then it became 10:30 and then 11:00 PM and they were still going strong. We had a new roommate who I was SURE was being bothered by all the noise and frankly, I was embarrassed.

The summer before this party, on the 4th of July during

the drought, the neighbor's nephew had sat across from our pasture in his mother's driveway shooting bottle rockets into our field! We pulled up in our vehicle and caught him, and of course he was drinking and belligerent, so my husband called the police department. The nephew didn't stick around to enforce his rights, he just left. But of course he told his mother and his uncle about this. We didn't think anything of the incident, because we knew we were in the right, so we dismissed it and forgot about it.   I mean, common sense would dictate that you don't shoot bottle rockets into someone's dry grass pasture during a drought, right?

Well, on that night Darryl was not home because he was working, it was dark and late and I was a little nervous. At 11:15 PM I went across the street to ask them to quiet down. They had been drinking for a while by now so all inhibitions were gone. They were enraged by my request to quiet down, told me that this was the country and they were allowed to party anytime they wanted and I had better just get used to it or move! The wife came screaming around the corner of their house, urging him to "Get her honey, Get her!" -- encouraging him to hurt me! He advanced toward me and got closer and closer to intimidate me. He said something to me about the incident with his nephew and the fireworks, and I immediately felt myself "go HULK"... I felt the Old Man rising up inside of me, and I was ready to go to battle in the flesh!

Even as I felt myself bowing up, ready to get in his face, I had the conscious thought process, "I CAN'T DO THIS! I am a Christian! I cannot get into an argument with this man!"

So, even though everything in me wanted to just duke it out with him right there in the middle of his driveway, came words from somewhere deep inside of me, "Obviously we have offended you, and I am sorry. I am very sorry that we have offended you. I really think we need to sit down and talk about this, and try to work things out."

I was so shocked! Who said that?

They were too drunk to notice, I'm sure they just thought I was a chicken, because after I said that they made fun of me about having offended them. I stuck it out for a few more minutes, but realized I was getting nowhere, so I left and walked across the street, still stunned that I had reacted like that to an obvious physical threat.

Darryl came home from work about 11:30 or 11:45. They had quieted down some around 11:30 but they were still outside in the yard with the music going and partying. I told him what happened, and he went down to the corner to get the policeman who he had passed on his way home. The policeman went across the street and they shut down for the night.

I was awakened to Love that night, when I realized I am

NOT my own. I had to act as Christ that night – I had no other choice! I had been awakened to LOVE.

There are so many other ways that I have been awakened to love, such as apologizing even when I know I'm right, but it's more important to not hurt the other person. It's being the ONLY ONE who cleans house, and never bringing it up. And a million, ZILLION other things that I now do, because I have Christ Jesus living inside of me.

Am I perfect? Not even close. But I am awakened to Perfection. And the Perfect has Come. Christ Jesus in me, the Hope of Glory!

He is alive in YOU, too! Awaken to the many ways that God is calling you to live and work in His Kingdom.

If you have questions or need some leadership in any of these areas, please contact me. I'll be happy to help!

Edie Bayer www.KingdomPromoters.org

ABOUT THE AUTHOR

Edie Bayer's primary focus is to promote and advance the Kingdom of God by helping people to hear and recognize the voice of the Lord, and then act upon it. Edie has served with international ministers Joan Hunter and Paulette Reed as well as Darren Canning and Dr. Judy Laird. Edie ministers as a Preacher and Prophet of God. She is an author, a speaker and itinerant minister.

Edie and her husband Darryl formed Kingdom Promoters (www.KingdomPromoters.org), to help further God's Kingdom by acting as an incubator to assist fledgling ministries in their start-up stages. Kingdom Promoters also hosts itinerant speakers and travelling ministers such as Dr. Linda Smith and Apostle William Dillon, as well as author Carol Sewell, among others.

You may reach Edie and Darryl at their website, www.KingdomPromoters.org and www.TexasBrass.com

Darryl Bayer has many CD's available on CDBaby.com and Amazon.com. You can find videos of them on YouTube.com

You may also read and sign up for Edie's blog, http://ediebear1.wordpress.com .

You may also wish to email Edie, ediebear1@gmail.com

Darryl and Edie are available to play, preach and prophesy at your church, ladies group or other event. Contact us!

Other titles by Edie Bayer:
1. Spiritual Espionage, Going Undercover for the Kingdom of God
2. Power Thieves, 7-Spirits that Steal Your Power and How to Get it Back!
3. Spiritual Lightning Rods, Connected to the Father of Lights
4. Narco, Awake O Sleeper
Watch for new book and music releases coming soon!

Edie and Darryl reside on a small homestead north of the Houston area. They raise chickens, ducks, quail and rabbits and have three cats. Edie has two children and three grandchildren.

Edie Bayer

www.ingramcontent.com/pod-product-compliance
Lightning Source LLC
Chambersburg PA
CBHW071853020426
42331CB00007B/1984